Distinctions in Nature

Reptiles and
Amphibians Explained

Shirley Duke

Cavendish
Square

New York

Published in 2017 by Cavendish Square Publishing, LLC
243 5th Avenue, Suite 136, New York, NY 10016

Copyright © 2017 by Cavendish Square Publishing, LLC

First Edition

Cataloging-in-Publication Data

Names: Duke, Shirley.
Title: Reptiles and amphibians explained / Shirley Duke.
Description: New York : Cavendish Square, 2017. | Series: Distinctions in nature | Includes index.
Identifiers: ISBN 9781502617774 (pbk.) | ISBN 9781502617460 (library bound) |
ISBN 9781502617606 (6 pack) | ISBN 9781502617521 (ebook)
Subjects: LCSH: Reptiles–Juvenile literature. | Amphibians–Juvenile literature.
Classification: LCC QL644.2 D87 2017 | DDC 597.9–dc23

Editorial Director: David McNamara
Editor: Kelly Spence
Copy Editor: Nathan Heidelberger
Art Director: Jeffrey Talbot
Designer: Stephanie Flecha
Production Assistant: Karol Szymczuk
Photo Research: J8 Media

The photographs in this book are used by permission and through the courtesy of: Achimdiver/Shutterstock.com, cover left; worldswildlifewonders/Shutterstock.com, cover right; Morphart Creation/Shutterstock.com, 4; reptiles4all/Shutterstock.com, 6; kriangsak hampitak/Shutterstock.com, 6; caecilian- FabioMaffei/iStock/Thinkstock, 7; John Cancalosi/National Geographic Magazines/Getty Images, 8; Dave King/Dorling Kindersley/Getty Images, 10; reptiles4all/Shutterstock.com, 11; Bob Elsdale/The Image Bank/Getty Images, 12; Jupiterimages/PHOTOS.com/Thinkstock.com, 14; Joanna K-V/Shutterstock.com, 15; Dorling Kindersley/Getty Images, 16; Steve Byland/Shutterstock.com, 16; Kazakova Maryia/Shutterstock.com, 17; Ryan M. Bolton/Shutterstock.com, 18; John Cancalosi/National Geographic Magazines/Getty Images, 18; Bruce Dale/National Geographic/Getty Images, 19; DAN SUZIO/Science Source/Getty Images, 20; Jim Merli/Visuals Unlimited/Getty Images, 20; Roger de la Harpe/Gallo Images/Getty Images, 22; almondd/Shutterstock.com, 22; Brian J. Skerry/National Geographic Magazines/Getty Images, 24; Tigerpython/File:Female Python sebae brooding eggs Tropicario, FIN.jpg/Wikimedia Commons, 26; Danita Delimont/Gallo Images/Getty Images, 26; R Degginger EScience Source/Getty Images, 27; Dave King/Dorling Kindersley/Getty Images, 27.

Printed in the United States of America

Contents

The axolotl, or Mexican salamander, is nicknamed the "walking fish." Some scientists believe that creatures like this show the ancient link between amphibians, reptiles, and fish.

Introduction: The Family Tree

Ancient **amphibians** were the first creatures to walk on dry land. Over time, some **species evolved** and became **reptiles**. The largest reptiles to ever walk the Earth were the dinosaurs. As more species continued to change, more groups formed. Animals like birds and **mammals** later descended from reptiles.

Scientists **classify**, or group, animals based on their similarities. Classifying living things into groups is called **taxonomy**. Some of these similarities are not easy to

As a reptile, a lizard (*right*) lives on land and is covered in dry scales. A salamander (*left*) is an amphibian. It can live on land, too, but only near wet places because of its soft, moist skin.

observe. In nature, many animals appear alike. A lizard looks similar to a salamander. But just because two animals look alike does not mean that they belong to the same group. A lizard is a reptile. A salamander is an amphibian.

Grouping Reptiles

There are about 8,700 different species of reptiles. They are classified in four **orders**, or groups: turtles and tortoises, snakes and lizards, crocodiles and

A caecilian's thick, pointed skull allows it to tunnel into the soil. This creature's sharp teeth help it catch food like worms, termites, and even frogs and lizards.

alligators, and **tuatara**. The tuatara is the last living species from an ancient group of reptiles. They look similar to lizards.

All Sorts of Amphibians

There are over 6,500 species of amphibians. They are divided into three orders: frogs and toads, salamanders and newts, and **caecilians**. Caecilians look like snakes and spend most of their lives underground. They live in warm, tropical places.

Like these western diamondback rattlesnakes, many snakes burrow into the ground to cool off when it is hot and to warm up when it is colder.

1 Reptiles and Amphibians

Reptiles and amphibians are often linked because they share common **traits**, or features. Both groups are **ectothermic**, or cold-blooded. This means they are unable to create heat inside their bodies. A cold-blooded animal takes in warmth from its surroundings to raise its body temperature. This allows its body to do everything it needs to live. If a cold-blooded animal becomes too warm, it must cool down by finding shade or **burrowing** into the ground.

This frog skeleton has a short, stiff backbone. A frog's backbone helps support the animal when it jumps.

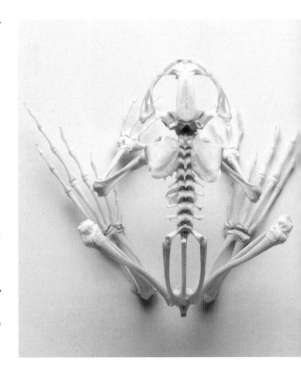

Reptiles and amphibians are also **vertebrates**. This means all animals in these two groups have a backbone. Even a snake has a spine running throughout its body. It uses muscles in its belly to slither along the ground.

All Shapes and Sizes

Reptiles come in all shapes and sizes. Some are large, like the Nile crocodile. Others are tiny, like the dwarf gecko. It is shorter than a finger in length. Examples of reptiles include the king snake, anole, and Gila monster.

Amphibians are generally smaller than reptiles. However, they are still a **diverse** group of animals. Bullfrogs, cane toads, and mole salamanders are all amphibians.

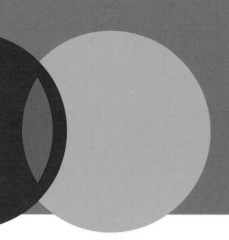

Zoom In

Scientists often study reptiles and amphibians together. This branch of science is called herpetology. Scientists often shorten this name and call them "herps."

The Gila monster is a poisonous lizard. Venom, a deadly liquid, is released from this reptile's teeth as it bites its prey.

A mother crocodile guards her newly hatched young.

2 Comparing Reptiles and Amphibians

As young, both reptiles and amphibians hatch from eggs. Each group has distinct differences in where they lay their eggs and what they look like.

Eggs on Land

Reptiles must lay their eggs on dry land. Some species lay only a few eggs at one time, while others lay hundreds. Most reptile eggs are protected by a stretchy, leathery shell. Others have a hard outer layer. Some species, like turtles, bury their eggs in an underground nest. They then leave the eggs

Zoom In

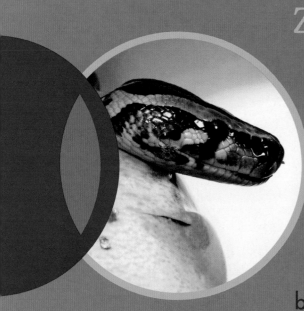

Some reptiles, like crocodiles and snakes, are born with an egg tooth. This special tooth helps the young to break through its shell while hatching. The egg tooth falls off or is reabsorbed by the animal's body as it grows.

to hatch on their own. Other reptiles, like crocodiles, guard their eggs until they hatch.

Life in the Water

Most amphibians lay many eggs—often hundreds or even thousands—at a time. Amphibian eggs do not have a shell. Instead, they are protected by a jelly-like sac. They

The jelly-like mass covering these frog eggs absorbs water and helps keep them from drying out. The tiny black specks are the newly developing frogs. They will eat the jelly as they grow.

are usually laid in water or another moist environment. If the eggs dry out, the young do not survive.

Let's Get Cracking

When a reptile is born, it looks like a smaller version of its parents. Most kinds of reptiles take at least one

This newly hatched grass snake comes out of its shell looking like a smaller version of its parents.

Young salamanders breathe through their gills.

year to fully grow. Amphibians usually take less time to mature.

Two Stages of Life

The word "amphibian" comes from two Greek words meaning "double life." Once an amphibian hatches, it spends the first part of its **life cycle** in the water. There, amphibians go through **metamorphosis**. This is a change in form that takes place as an animal grows.

All amphibians are born with **gills**. These little slits allow them to breathe underwater. Some of them later **adapt** and develop lungs. Others keep gills for their

A frog lays a clump of eggs in a jelly-like sac. Tiny tadpoles hatch from the eggs. As they grow, they develop legs and lungs. They no longer need their gills to breathe and can live on land.

Frog life cycles differ from species to species. Their surroundings, like the temperature and how much water is present, affect how the animals grow.

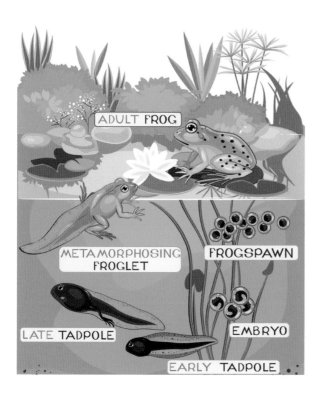

whole life. It can take up to five years for some amphibians to fully develop.

Body Armor

All reptiles are covered in hard, dry

This alligator snapping turtle does not outgrow its shell. Instead, it sheds its scutes as it grows.

A snake sheds the outer layer of its skin, revealing a fresh layer of skin beneath.

scales, even if they are hard to see. A reptile's scales help lock in moisture. This is especially important in dry places, like a desert. A turtle's thick shell is made of **scutes**, a thin covering of scales over bony plates.

Reptiles **molt**, or shed, their scales. Some reptiles, like snakes, shed their scales in one piece. Others, like lizards, slowly lose their old scales over a few days. New scales grow underneath to replace the old ones.

Smooth Skin

Amphibians have much thinner skin than reptiles. It feels soft and moist to the touch. They are able to breathe and take in water through their skin. These

A reptile's scales are made of keratin. This is the same strong material that your hair and nails are made of. Water cannot pass through keratin. Reptiles like sea snakes and crocodiles live in salt water. Their scales protect them from the salty environment.

animals are mostly found in moist, wet environments because their skin does not offer much protection against **dehydration**. They produce a special **mucus** to protect their skin. Like reptiles, amphibians also shed their skin. But instead of leaving it behind, most amphibians eat the dead skin.

Frogs and toads like this cane toad shed their skin regularly. They push the whole piece of skin off with their back legs and move the shed skin under their tongues to swallow it.

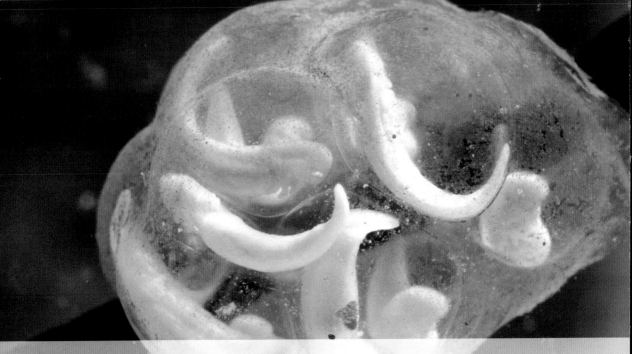

1. These developing young are about eleven days old.

2. Kingsnakes live all over the United States.

3 Be an Animal Detective

Test your skills and see if you can identify which of these animals (*left*) are reptiles and which ones are amphibians.

1. These tiny creatures will be born in water. As they grow up, they will change form. When they hatch, which group will they belong to?

2. This animal is covered in hard scales. It will shed its skin in one long piece. Is this a reptile or an amphibian?

3. Crocodiles fiercely guard their nests and will roll the eggs using their mouths to help the young hatch.

4. Young salamanders, called efts, take cover under rotting logs or damp leaves when it is dry out.

3. A mother laid these eggs in a nice, dry nest. She
   will stay nearby to guard her eggs until they hatch.
   Is she a reptile or an amphibian?

4. This little animal has gills but also breathes through
   its skin, which must remain moist. Is it a reptile or
   an amphibian?

Answer Key:

1. These are newt young. Newts are amphibians. The
   young will undergo metamorphosis and then be
   able to live on land.

2. Kingsnakes are reptiles. In the wild, these snakes
   will eat almost any animal they can swallow whole.

3. Nile crocodiles are reptiles that live in large rivers,
   swamps, and lakes. They can eat up to half their
   body weight at one time.

4. These young salamanders are amphibians. They
   live on land at this stage of their life. Efts can be
   bright red or orange.

The leatherback sea turtle has adapted to keep its body temperature warm by staying active and having a thick layer of fat and a large body.

4 ● Rule Breakers

Some species of reptiles and amphibians stand out and are unique in their groups.

Leatherback Sea Turtle

The leatherback sea turtle is a reptile. However, unlike other reptiles, these animals have some control over their body temperature. Their blood supply goes to their bones. This lets their body temperature stay a bit warmer than the water temperature. At this temperature, most reptiles could not be active.

A female boa constrictor rests after giving birth because the eggs growing inside her require most of her energy.

Hellbenders like clear, fast-moving water. If these animals are around, the water is of good quality.

Boa Constrictor

A few reptiles, like a boa constrictor, give birth to live young instead of laying eggs. Female boas carry the eggs inside their bodies, where they hatch. The babies are then born live from their mother. Boa constrictors can give birth to up to sixty babies at one time. The newborns are about 2 feet (0.6 meters) long.

Different Salamanders

The giant salamander and the hellbender, a 2-foot- (61-centimeter-) long salamander, spend their entire lives in the water. While these two species develop

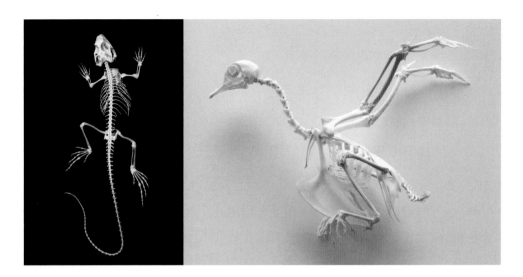

Scientists have observed many similarities between the skeletons of reptiles and birds.

lungs, they rarely use them to breathe. Instead, they breathe through their skin and use their lungs to help them float in water.

Birds

Based on fossils, scientists have learned that birds and crocodiles are more closely related to each other than lizards are to snakes. Birds developed over time from reptiles. Recent discoveries in China of two different feathered dinosaur species support this idea.

adapt To change over a long period of time.

amphibians Cold-blooded animals with smooth, moist skin that lay eggs in water and go through two stages of development, one in water and one on land.

burrowing Digging a hole or tunnel.

caecilians Tropical amphibians that look like a smooth snake or worm.

classify To put into groups based on similarities.

dehydration The process of losing bodily fluid.

diverse Very different; having lots of variety.

ectothermic Describing an animal that depends on its surroundings to regulate its body temperature.

evolved Developed slowly as a species over time to a more complex form.

gills Small slits in the neck area of some animals that allow them to breathe underwater.

herpetology The branch of science that studies reptiles and amphibians.

keratin The material found in the scales of reptiles that is made of the same material as hair and fingernails.

life cycle The stages of life that a living thing undergoes from its birth to its death.

mammals Animals with fur that give birth to live young. The young feed on their mothers' milk.

metamorphosis A change from one thing to another, such as a tadpole changing to a frog.

molt To shed skin as an animal grows.

mucus A thick, protective liquid.

orders Groups used to classify living things.

reptiles Cold-blooded animals covered with scales that lay eggs.

scutes The thin, outer plates that cover the bony shell of some reptiles.

species A group of animals that share common traits.

taxonomy The science of putting living things with like traits into groups.

traits Characteristics of a living thing.

tuatara A reptilian species that is lizard-like and lives on islands near New Zealand.

vertebrates Animals that have backbones.

Books

Berger, Melvin, and Gilda Berger. *Scholastic True or False: Amphibians.* New York: Scholastic, 2011.

Kay, Ann. *100 Facts on Reptiles & Amphibians.* 100 Facts. Essex, UK: Miles Kelly, 2015.

Wilsdon, Christina. *Ultimate Reptileopedia: The Most Complete Reptile Reference Ever.* Washington, DC: National Geographic Kids, 2015.

Websites

National Geographic Kids: Amphibians
kids.nationalgeographic.com/animals/hubs/amphibians
Explore the watery world of amphibians.

National Geographic Kids: Reptiles
kids.nationalgeographic.com/animals/hubs/reptiles
Learn about animals that fall into the reptile order.

Index

Page numbers in **boldface** are illustrations.

Shirley Duke has written more than fifty books about science and nature, but writing about life science is her specialty. She has studied reptiles in the field and seen them up close, but has observed a few amphibians as well. A resident of the Jemez Mountains in New Mexico, she learned about the endangered Jemez salamander and what is being done to protect it.